The Little Book of Thunks®

260 questions to make your brain go ouch!

Ian Gilbert

Crown House Publishing Limited
www.crownhouse.co.uk
www.crownhousepublishing.com

First published by

Crown House Publishing Ltd
Crown Buildings, Bancyfelin, Carmarthen, Wales, SA33 5ND, UK
www.crownhouse.co.uk

and

Crown House Publishing Company LLC
6 Trowbridge Drive, Suite 5, Bethel, CT 06801, USA
www.crownhousepublishing.com

© Ian Gilbert 2007

Thunks® and **THUNKS**® are the registered trademarks of
Independent Thinking Ltd.

Published 2007. Reprinted 2007, 2008 (twice), 2009, 2010, 2013, 2015.

British Library Cataloguing-in-Publication Data
A catalogue entry for this book is available
from the British Library.

13-digit ISBN 978-184590062-5

LCCN 2007920937

Printed and bound in the UK by
Gomer Press, Llandysul, Ceredigion

To Olivia

For being so determined to succeed

Contents

Acknowledgments

Many thanks to Mike and Pam Cousins and all the teachers involved in Northamptonshire's groundbreaking Raising Standards Partnership, especially Celia James at Kingsbrook School.

And a big thank you to all the children and students who have let me walk into their lives and make their brains hurt.

Part I

The Origins and Uses of Thunks

Philosophy is what's left when science
has answered all the other questions

What is a *Thunk*?

A *Thunk* is a beguilingly simple-looking question about everyday things that stops you in your tracks and helps you start looking at the world in a whole new light. At the same time it encourages you to engage in verbal fisticuffs with the people sitting next to you and, if used properly, always leads to severe brain ache.[1]

The *Thunks* in this book cover areas of human existence, including truth, justice, reality, beliefs, the natural world, the human condition, art, beauty, right and wrong, good and bad, life and death, war, religion, love, friendship and whether Marmite tastes nice.

Any one *Thunk* can start to help people see that all communication is riddled with potholes that, just maybe, we need to look out for including intentions, definitions, presuppositions, opinions, assumptions, approximations, biases, prejudices, non sequiturs, and everything else that happens when a politician's lips move.

What's more, 'thunk' is also the noise the brain makes when it starts to think about a *Thunk* and, as such, is the one of the first onomatopoeias to provide hours of endless fun since Ker-Plunk.

---

[1] Some people may try and tell you that a 'thunk' is 'computer code that performs a translation or conversion during a call or indirection' but don't listen to them. They are probably the same sort of people who will attempt to persuade you that 'debugging flat thunks generated by the thunk compiler can be difficult because the thunk mechanism is complex and debugging tools capable of tracing through thunks are difficult to use' and, as such, should be avoided.

What is a *Thunk* for?

It is easy to go through life without ever lifting it up, giving it a shake and looking at it from a different angle. When we do this we start to realise that what we thought were facts are actually opinions, what we took to be knowledge is actually supposition, and not everything you read in *Daily Mail* is true. A *Thunk* will help you to look with new eyes at everyday occurrences such as the wind, broken-down cars, and things that are black. And, by helping you to look deeper and question harder, may even help you to get more out of life – which is a big claim for a little book – but such is the power of *Thunks*.

In the words of one eight-year-old boy after his first session, "I've just realised how big life is."

Where do *Thunks* come from?

There is a thinking skills programme that originated in the US called *Philosophy for Children* – known by those in a hurry as *P4C* – that has a growing following in the UK. A professor of philosophy named Matthew Lipman realised that his students could tell you what philosophers such as Socrates or Plato thought but couldn't think for themselves. Which is a bit like putting your trunks on to read a book about swimming. He put together a series of stories and a special way of working that could be used with children of all ages to help them develop a more philosophical way of thinking. *Thunks* grew out of my work in this area with children in primary and secondary schools (and even tax inspectors) and are a way of quickly and easily getting people thinking and talking philosophically.

How does a *Thunk* work?

Socrates was a clever man and a teacher who would help his students simply by asking questions, something we now call a 'Socratic dialogue'. Through questioning in this way, people will either develop a more profound and reasoned appreciation of why what they feel to be true is true or untrue, or else may end up no longer really knowing what a tree is. Could go either way.

Although the idea of using questions to generate thinking goes back thousands of years, even great recent philosophers such as Wittgenstein have suggested that a perfectly respectable philosophical essay could comprise entirely of questions. Or jokes. Or both. He also knew the benefits to thinking of laughter and once asked the wonderful *Thunk*, "Why don't dogs simulate pain? Is it because they are too honest?"

What are the benefits of *Thunks*?

Check out a list of famous Swiss people and somewhere between Theophrastus Bombastus von Hohenheim and Ursula Andress you will find the name Jean Piaget.

Many present day insights into childhood development come from his observations and theories from the last century – theories that can now be backed up by neuroscience, despite having been dismissed at one time or another.[2] It was Piaget who suggested that – and I urge you to copy this line out and stick it in a place where you'll see it daily – "Intelligence is what you use when you don't know what to do." *Thunks* tap into this definition of intelligence and help us move away from the idea that the intelligent person is the one with the good memory and a grasp of basic grammar. (If you don't believe me, listen to *Brain of Britain* on BBC Radio 4 – it's a memory game of abstruse facts, and nothing to do with the application of knowledge in new environments. I bet few of the winners over the last decade could fix a Fiesta headlight with a courgette as someone I know once did.)

I was once asked to 'motivate' a conference of tax inspectors who were coming to terms with the fact that the Inland Revenue and HM Customs and Excise were being combined into one large organisation – HM Revenue & Customs. (Before I went, I typed 'motivated tax inspectors' onto Google™ and received the reply, "Your search returned no documents.") These were people at the top of their tree for whom the world was soon to be unlike it had ever been previously. They were going to be asked questions that had never been asked before and were expected to come up

---

[2] Neuroscience spends a lot of time catching up with good practice when it comes to children, with parents and teachers greeting the findings of many multi-million dollar research projects with a resounding 'Well, duh!'

with answers – answers that couldn't be found in books, on websites, or in anyone's brain. I took them through a number of *Thunks* for precisely the reason that Piaget explains.

In a similar vein, someone once told me an Oxbridge admissions tutor was asked how they differentiated between A grade A-level students who are clever and A grade A-level students who have been well schooled and have a good memory. "Easy," the tutor replied, "I simply ask them a question no one's ever asked them before."

In a school setting *Thunks* are not only useful as a discrete thinking skills activity, they can also be used in all areas of the curriculum, for example, at the beginning of a new topic. One science teacher was going to use *Thunks* such as, "If your doctor knew you had a gene that meant you would die at 25, would you want her to tell you? Should she tell you anyway? Would you want anyone else to know?" as a lead into the part of the curriculum covering genetics and Human Genome Project. Similarly, some of the wonderful discussions I have had with children starting from the simplest of *Thunks* – Is black a colour? – would lead perfectly into science, art or even citizenship lessons.

A maths teacher was once berating me for suggesting that philosophical thought could be useful in his area where, as far as he was concerned, there were no grey areas and the answer to a mathematical question either was or it wasn't. I tried to point out that maths and philosophy go back a long way, reminding him that above Plato's door was written "Only geometers may enter here", but he was having none of it. He asked me (I say asked, maybe 'goaded' is a better word) to come up with an example so I put to him the question, "What's a third of love?" – a question he was singularly unable to answer. Yet I have subsequently put it to many people, young and old, who are able to identify a whole range of valid responses including trust, kissing, 'luh...!' and, controversially, foreplay. (My favourite one was 'toothpaste' – this from a girl whose parents had split up but had recently reconciled, the first sign of which was the father leaving a toothbrush back at the mother's house again.)

Along with huge curriculum benefits there are many generic skills being developed when children work in this way, including:

- thinking
- listening
- talking
- hypothesising
- arguing
- team working
- decision making
- evaluating
- weighing pros and cons
- analysing
- presenting
- selling
- persuading
- changing your mind

- mental agility
- self control
- discussion
- debate
- learning to enjoy intellectual challenge
- dealing with doubt and uncertainty
- thinking quickly and under pressure
- realising that there is often more than one answer
- realising there are sometimes no answers at all
- realising that different people look at the world in different ways
- learning that it's ok to not think what everyone else thinks
- learning to be confident in your own thoughts
- learning to laugh

Not only that, such work can also have a huge positive impact on self-esteem (and as one famous philosopher, Spinoza, once said, "Self-esteem is the highest thing we can hope for"). One of the first student groups I worked with in this way were a dozen or so children referred to by their head of year as 'the lost boys and girls'. These were children who were shy, quiet and reserved, never really entering any teacher's radar. Through their *P4C* work this group really came to life, becoming more confident in lessons, leading philosophy lunches for their teachers, running a whole school INSET session on why they wanted more opportunities for *P4C* in their lessons, setting up a philosophy website (see page 93), leading sessions in local primary schools, speaking at national conferences and even appearing on BBC Radio 4 and Teachers' TV.

Not bad for a group of quiet children.

Every time I go into a school to model a *P4C* lesson with a group of children observed by their teachers I always end up with the situation where one particular child, who hasn't said a word in class for months, is the one who holds forth and really comes into their own. It makes you wonder how many children go through their school lives not joining in out of sheer fear of getting it 'wrong'. Take being right or wrong out of the equation and you are just left with thoughts and everyone has those.[3]

Another benefit relates to what I call 'pull' motivation (as opposed to 'push' motivation). By tapping into a child's natural curiosity and engaging in questions, children start to pull towards them answers and learning compared to a traditional classroom model of a teacher providing answers to a series of questions the child has not even thought about. In one session with a group of 14 year olds I had put the *Thunk*, "Is there more future or past?" One girl suggested that, if you believe in the afterlife, there was indeed more future. In the true style of Socratic dialogue I probed further, "What if you don't believe in the after-life?" to which she replied, after some thought, that there was still more future anyway. "So, whether you believe in the afterlife or not there's still more future?" I put to her. "Yes" came the confident reply, at which point a lad next

---

[3] Interestingly, I often find the 'bright' child who is normally the one first to have their hand up in the 'guess what's in the teacher's head' game has the most problems working under the new rules where, infuriatingly, there is nothing at all in the teacher's head.

to me suddenly burst out with the memorable question, "So, what's the point of religion then?" He will now go in to a religious studies lesson with a different mindset because he is beginning to ask questions that in turn will lead him to seek answers. (And this is one of the most fundamental questions being asked in the 21st century – just ask Richard Dawkins.)

One infant school from a statistically disadvantaged area in the Midlands realised that, after exploring *P4C* for a day, the children were having trouble formulating questions of their own. They then set about a wonderful school-wide project to encourage questions including a Question Tree in reception and a Book of Questions that they added to whenever they started a new topic. Questions such as "Do magnets work under water?" are fairly straightforward to answer (just ask those US Navy-enlisted dolphins), but as a starting point for the topic on 'forces' leads to a wholly more satisfying educational experience for all concerned.

How do you use a *Thunk*?

Some people have used *Thunks* sitting at the dinner table, some use them with their children in the car on the way back from swimming, some have used them waiting for the pub to open.

Mostly they are used by sitting a group of between 10 and 30 children in a circle – something Lipman refers to as a *Community of Enquiry*.

(If you are doing this in a school setting, some words of warning for the teacher in you – working in this way is not about 'teaching' them anything, something that is by definition the process of getting them to think your thoughts. *Philosophy for Children* is about helping them develop their own thinking which means you must step back and refrain from:

- teaching
- correcting anything they say which you may feel is not true
- telling them they are either right or wrong
- giving a definitive answer
- showing how clever and knowledgeable you are
- getting them to guess what's in your head
- telling them off for getting excited or chatty
- finishing their answers for them
- insisting that they 'join in' by talking to the group[4]
- diving in and 'rescuing' the group if a question is met with silence – silence is a good thing when you ask a question
- waiting for no more than two seconds once a question has been asked before giving them an answer or, worse, another question

---

[4] Just because they are not talking doesn't mean to say they are not joining in. Far from it. Sometimes those who speak most think least. It's the same in the pub.

- telling them not to be stupid or silly
- disagreeing with them
- resolving issues
- moralising
- proving a point
- or, indeed, anything else that will get in the way of letting children feel confident to play with ideas, to interact, to join in, to feel secure and to get the best out of the session.)

Socratic dialogue, if you remember, is all about asking questions. Your skill – and one that you are modelling for children to develop too – is to reply to people's hypotheses with questions that lead them into evaluating their thoughts deeper to see if they really hold water. Sometimes, you can just take their view of reality and extend it until it either holds up or explodes. For example, one nine-year-old girl had suggested that a broken-down car was parked if the handbrake was on and the keys were out of the ignition. "What about if that was the case but you then dropped it out of an aeroplane? Would it still be parked then?" was a way to push that hypothesis to its limits. "Or what about if it was broken down with its handbrake on and the keys out, but was on the back of car transporter travelling down the motorway? Could you travel at 60 miles an hour in broken-down parked car?"

Similarly, there was the boy (and I must say, plenty of adults too) who was citing the 'grape from Tesco's defence' when asked the *Thunk* about whether reading a paper in a newsagent qualified as stealing. "That's just testing," he said confidently. "OK," said the Socrates in me, "What about two grapes?" "Testing," was his still confident reply. "Three grapes?" "Testing" was still the reply, but with slightly less assurance now. Time for the killer blow: "Four grapes?" "No," he replied, "that would be stealing." Other equally useful responses could have included, "What if you ate the fourth grape first?" or "What if you don't like grapes and took them home for someone else to test?"

There is a frustration in some children when you challenge their logic with your 'extreme logic' ("You're just looking for an argument, sir!"), but it is a frustration born out of the inadequacies in their own thinking when they realise that not really thinking things through is no longer good enough. As long as the session is led in an atmosphere of good-humoured honesty and equality, children seem well able to take being challenged in this way.

There is also a contagiousness about such thinking which can spread through a school and into family homes in a matter of hours, as was the case when the *Thunk*, "If I put a bunch of flowers in the back of a computer does it become a vase?" was first put to the 'lost boys and girls'. There was hardly a student, teacher or parent who had not had that question put to them within a day of it being first being put to the group.

Above all, remember a *Thunk* is merely a starting point, a catalyst for thinking. That's all. One teacher used *Thunks* with small special needs groups where she referred to them as 'thought hand grenades' – something you just lob into a group and sit back and watch how it really gets people's brains going. You may start by asking whether a bird's nest is art, but within a few moments that conversation has hairpinned into whether a lightbulb is heavier when it's on. Although you may want to steer it at times if you are using *Thunks* as part of a specific lesson, on the whole it's best just see where they go.

Think of it as a voyage of discovery from A to A.

What does a good *Thunk* session look like?

Once you are comfortable and in a circle (or a huddle) and have explained that in this session there are no rights or wrongs nor will they be doing any reading or writing[5], it often good to warm up the brain with a few Possibly Impossible Questions – questions for which there is no 'right' answer but where everyone has an answer and can justify it. Questions such as:

- What colour is Tuesday/shopping/happiness/maths ...?
- Which is heavier – rich or poor/happiness or sadness/ light or dark ...?

---

[5] This usually met by quiet clenched fists of joy by the boys in the group. Again, this makes you wonder how often children – some boys especially – refrain from thinking in the classroom. Traditionally, the more they think the more they end up having to write so if they don't think very much they won't have to write very much. This is backed up by how good some of the most disaffected boys are at dealing with *Thunks* and how much they seem to enjoy it.

- Is there more happiness or sadness/things or space/ pebbles or blades of grass in the world ...?
- The answer is six/never/once with a fish ... – what's the question?
- If pigs/elephants/fish ... ruled the world what changes would we see?[6]
- What do a dog/vacuum cleaner/baseball cap and a history/maths/science lesson have in common?
- What do you get if you cross a rabbit/politician/head-teacher/fish with a car/hat/cabbage/pencil sharpener?

... that sort of thing.

Apart from getting the brain switched on to think laterally right from the start (and, as such, are so much more effective than the traditional exhortation, "Come on children – think outside the box"), such questions also help to reinforce the idea that there really are no right or wrong answers, something children sometimes take a while to trust you on.

A circle – Lipman's *Community of Enquiry* – is important. It sends the message that we are all equal (think King Arthur rather than Alan Sugar). That said, feel free to have the participants moving around at times too. This may be something simple like asking the whole group to stand up, get a bit of air in their lungs, do a bit of excercise (check out *Smart Moves* in the Bibliography for more information about this) and then ask all those who

---

[6] One group memorably identified that if zebras ruled the world there would be no racism.

think of one answer to a *Thunk* to sit down, the rest to remain standing. Another version is to get all those who think one particular answer to sit at one side of the circle, those with another answer to go and sit on another side.[7] At any time they can change their mind and cross the circle to go and join another group. This is a great test of the confi-dence a child has in his or her own thoughts, especially when everyone else is over on the other side of the circle and they are standing alone. It is a wonderful moment to see that 'quiet' child stand up for what they alone think is right and then manage to persuade other people to change their minds and join them.

Sometimes you may put a *Thunk* to the whole group and treat it as a traditional hands-up question and answer exercise. Sometimes you may give them a question but refuse to consider any hands up until a minute's thinking time has elapsed. Sometimes you may get them to think through their responses in pairs or threes for 60 seconds or so. You can also get them to put forward the *Thunks* so you can move away from being the person leading the sessions. Play around with the format to keep things lively and buzzing.

---

[7] It is always best to have 'other' as one of the potential responses when it comes to answering a *Thunk*. This gives space for people to come up with responses you had never even thought of and is also better than 'I don't know' which can be used as an intellectual cop-out. After all, you're not asking them what they 'know' but what they 'think'.

Can you have too much of good *Thunk*?

With small children you may just do a session of 10 minutes or so; with older ones maybe up to an hour. I have
been involved in *P4C* sessions with primary children that
have gone on productively for nearly two hours although
that may have been something to do with the fact that
they were missing science at the time. Some schools use
Philosophy for Children as a discrete thinking skills 'slot' and
do it, say, every Friday afternoon. Others use it as part of
a philosophy club at lunchtimes. Others still are using
them to replace the traditional 'thought for the week'.
After all, a thought – and someone else's thought at that
– can be a full stop whereas a question is a starting point.

Some teachers use it formally for an entire lesson, others
use it as a tool part way through a lesson, just dropped in
to get children going. The more you do it the more you'll
get a feel for how often to do it, when to stop and what
good it's doing. Always be prepared to drop a *Thunk* and
move on to another one at any time. Don't think that you
have to follow one through until you have covered every
line of thought (i.e. never flog a dead *Thunk*). Swapping
from one *Thunk* to another very quickly is fine and adds
energy and a sense of surprise to the session. Some of the
boys especially seem to like this way of working. Having
to move from thinking about the nature of time and
existence as you ponder whether there is more future or
past, to having suddenly to get your brain around whether
you weigh less once you have passed wind, is a great test
of mental agility and an exercise in neural aerobics that

has got to be a useful practice for an ever-changing, lightning-speed, multi-tasking, portfolio-working 21st century world.

What can cause a session of *Thunks* not to go well?

The biggest challenge to a productive session of *Thunks* is where the participants still think there are right or wrong answers despite the teacher's protestations. This is why a few minutes of warm up is essential in setting the scene. Being too 'teacher-like' can also squash philosophical thought (see list on pages 15/16). If a child puts forward a 'silly' answer don't judge it, just ask him (it is usually a 'him' in my experience) to explain and justify it. Or else rephrase it back to him: "So, what you're saying is ...?" – in such a way that it sounds like a clever question. I find they soon learn.

The subject of discipline can be one that is best addressed by the *Community of Enquiry* as a whole. If the group sets its own standards of behaviour then the group – and not the teacher – can also administer punishments to those breaking those rules.

Some teachers have used various Circle Time approaches to managing listening and speaking, such as you can only speak when you have hold of the 'White Feather of Eloquence' or the 'Great Marker Pen of Verbosity'. One inner-city English teacher used two different coloured tennis balls – the orange one had to be in your possession before you could join in to agree with a point, the yellow one was for arguing.

Although it can be done with full class groups (including moving the tables around in the time allocated) it may be that you are working with a group that you feel is just too big. If so, again, play around with format. One English teacher I worked with in a secondary school followed up my initial work with the whole class by grouping them into four separate circles whenever she wanted to do *P4C* work. Another variation is to have two concentric circles. The outer group could be recording the ideas and thoughts of the inner group for later evaluation. You could even play tag where children work in pairs, one in the circle, one outside, but only the one in the circle can speak.

From an age point of view *P4C* has been successfully used with children of all ages from nursery onwards, including considerable success in special schools. You will see that, of the *Thunks* here, some are more relevant for older children, some for younger ones. Feel free to adapt the *Thunk* to match the age range you are working with, and remember, even young children enjoy talking about – and arguably benefit from having the opportunity to talk about – areas including love and hate, life and death.

Sometimes a *Thunk* may actually lead nowhere in terms of discussion and debate. Everyone suddenly agrees that, for example, yes, a dog does know it's a dog, why are you asking such a stupid question, can we move on now and never talk of it ever again. If that happens, stay calm, smile and simply throw another one into the pot. There's plenty here.

How do you end a good session of *Thunks*?

Drawing on Professor Lipman's model for *Philosophy for Children*, I always end a session by giving the group 30 seconds to think of one sentence to sum up what's been going through their heads over the last 10 minutes/40 minutes/hour ... Then we go round the group to hear everyone's sentence (giving people the opportunity to 'pass' if they want to). Such an exercise brings closure to the session, ensures everyone can have the 'final word' and allows the teacher/facilitator the opportunity to see what has been going on in people's heads during the session. This is especially rewarding when you hear some amazingly well thought out and insightful comment from a child who hasn't said a word during the entire session.

How do you know the *Thunks* have been worthwhile?

The ultimate testament to a great session is the phrase, "My brain hurts" (although, "What the @$%! was that all about?!" has been known too). One 'naughty' nine-year-old girl's phrase was "People say I haven't got a brain – but that can't be true because it hurts."

Is there life after *Thunks*?

Enjoy playing around with the *Thunks* in this little book and feel free to come up with some of your own (see my website forum www.thunks.co.uk). And if you would like to learn more about *Philosophy for Children* then contact SAPERE who will tell you more about the training they offer. Details are on page 93.

Teaching children to think quickly, deeply and with agility has got to be one of the greatest gifts we can offer them as they take their place as adults in the 21st century. Ironic really that an intellectual process dating back thousands of years may be the best chance we have to deal with what the future has in store for us.

When an individual can combine those mental skills with the confidence and self-esteem to believe in the validity of their own thoughts, to speak their mind eloquently (and change it intelligently when they have to), to challenge poor thinking and prejudice confidently and with conviction (and not just in the *Daily Mail*), and to enjoy the cut and thrust of mental challenge, then surely we can say we have done the best job we could have done.

And a *Thunk* is a little word with a big part to play in such hugely important challenge.

Part II

The
Thunks

"I'm not looking for answers that
make the questions go away"
– *Australian rabbi*

1. If I borrow a million pounds am I a millionaire?

2. If you were identified as being genetically inclined to do bad things should you be locked up before you do them?

3. *If I say 'I have a pound' (because I felt a pound coin in my pocket) but when I take it out it's actually a button, but then I find a pound (in another pocket), was I right or wrong in saying 'I have a pound' in the first place?*

4. Could you invent a time machine that moved you forward in time at one minute per minute?

5. *Does your dog/cat/horse love you the way you love it?*

6. A wise man once said, "Love – and do as you wish." Would that be a good way to lead a life?

7. Could you pretend to love someone? If you were good at it, would they ever know you were just pretending?

8. Which would be worse – a world without love or a world full of hate (or are they the same thing)?

9. Could a fly cause an aeroplane to crash?

10. *Is there more future or past?*

11. Can you be 'best friends' with more than one person? If so, what is the maximum number of best friends you can have?

12. Can you have a friend you don't like?

13. Would you rather be a brave fool or a clever coward?

14. *Which is more important, being right or being nice?*

15. Are heroes ever scared?

16. CAN HATING MAKE YOU HAPPY?
MORE SUCCESSFUL?

17. CAN YOU CHOOSE
WHO TO LOVE? CAN
YOU CHOOSE NOT
TO LOVE SOMEONE?

18. *Is it worse to slap a child or torture a cat?*

19. <u>CAN YOU EVER REALLY FORGIVE AND FORGET?</u>

20. Does a mouse have a soul? A wasp? An amoeba?

21. If you say sorry but don't mean it, but the person you are apologising to thinks you are genuine, does it still count?

22. *Should we thank our parents for our being who we are?*

23. CAN YOU EVER BE GRATEFUL FOR BAD THINGS HAPPENING?

24. Should you be made to be polite?

25. IS IT EVER RIGHT TO BULLY A BULLY?

26. Is it ever right to 'blow your own trumpet'?

27. DOES A SOUND EXIST?

28. Is not being against racism the same as being for it?

29. *Would you rather live under democracy or a dictatorship led by Father Christmas?*

30. *If being brave is a good thing, does that mean that daring criminals are at least partly good?*

31. IS ANYTHING WORTH DYING FOR?

32. Do you think people with a serious illness are brave (as the press often describes them)?

33. Would you rather be brave and poor or cowardly and rich?

34. If you see someone being bullied should you do anything about it? If you don't should you feel guilty?

35. IF A RABBIT SUDDENLY RAN IN FRONT OF MY CAR SHOULD I FEEL GUILTY FOR HITTING IT?

36. *Can you ever really know what it's like to be someone else?*

37. IS TAKING PITY ON SOMEONE A GOOD THING?

38. Can a baby commit a crime? What about a dog?

39. Does a newborn baby love its mother?

40. If you could take a pill that would make you always happy, would you?

41. *If you could take a pill that meant you would never fail, would you?*

42. If I have a pig's heart valve implanted in my heart am I part pig? Am I more pig-like than someone without it?

43. If scientists can create living things that are part animal, part human is such a thing more human than a 'baby' in the womb that is just two cells big?

44. WOULD YOU HAVE YOUR SENSE OF HUMOUR REMOVED FOR A MILLION POUNDS?

45. Is black a colour?

46. If I switch the lights off does the wall change colour?

47. Can you cast a shadow into a dark room?

48. In a dark room what does a mirror reflect? If nothing, does that mean the mirror is not working?

49. Can you touch the wind?

50. <u>Can you touch a rainbow?</u>

51. IS A BROKEN-DOWN CAR PARKED?

52. Is there more happiness or sadness in the world?

53. CAN YOU FEEL HAPPY AND SAD AT THE SAME TIME?

54. *If I read a comic in a shop without paying for it is that stealing?*

55. IF I SWAP YOUR PEN FOR ONE EXACTLY THE SAME WITHOUT TELLING YOU IS THAT STEALING?

56. *If I pick up your pen by mistake and put it in my bag is that stealing?*

57. If you ask me if I have your pen and I say no because I mistakenly don't think I have, is that lying?

58. If I ask if I can steal your pen and you say yes, is that stealing?

59. <u>If we borrow every single book from a library is it still a library?</u>

60. If we move the entire school and everything and everybody in it to Africa would it still be the same school?

61. If we took the school building and moved it to the other side of town but left the people and things exactly where they were, where would the school be?

62. DOES LINED PAPER WEIGH MORE THAN BLANK PAPER?

63. *Did Theseus 'cheat' in the labyrinth?*

64. Is it ever OK to cheat?

65. Can I cheat if I don't know the rules?

66. Is a computer clever?

67. *If I go somewhere in my car directed by sat nav who directed me there?*

68. IS THE GAP BETWEEN THE NOTES MUSIC?

69. Is all sound music?

70. If I wrote a piece of music down but never played it is it music?

71. If I hit a triangle once is that music? What about if I hit it a million times?

72. Would you give money to a busker playing a triangle? What if they were playing the triangle part of Mozart's greatest work?

73. *If we end up without enough water for all the people in the world, is that because there is not enough water or too many people?*

74. If I swapped hearts with you would you still be you and me still me? What about brains? Faces? Lives?

75. If I met you a year ago in a building that has now been knocked down, where is the spot where I met you now?

76. If it's zero degrees today and tomorrow will be twice as cold, what temperature will it be tomorrow?

77. IS BUTTER MAN-MADE OR NATURAL? WHAT ABOUT PLASTIC (WHICH COMES FROM OIL, WHICH COMES ULTIMATELY FROM TREES)?

78. Are you man-made or natural?

79. What's the opposite of 'truth'? 'Love'? 'Life?'

80. Could the Rolling Stones do a Rolling Stones tribute band?

81. If every member of the Rolling Stones changed except one, would it still be the Rolling Stones? What if just one member changed? If the Rolling Stones changed their name to the Rolling Scones and kept all the same members – who would they be then?

82. *If I took the body off a car would it still be a car? What if I took all the wheels off instead? Removed the engine?*

83. Which is heavier, an inflated or deflated balloon?

84. *If the water in the river changes all the time what or where exactly is the river?*

85. Can a square be ugly? A dog? A chaffinch?

86. Can you think of anything that can't be ugly?

87. What colour would be a zebra be if you took its stripes off?

88. Is a millionaire who is marooned on a desert island still a millionaire?

89. If I had a million pounds and bought a million-pound house would I still be a millionaire?

90. What if I spent a million pounds on food and ate it all up?

91. *If someone is begging for money and I don't give them any and so, to prevent themselves from starving, they managed to get a job and in a few years were rich – have I been nicer to them than the person who gave them a pound?*

92. If I gave a beggar a pound would that be encouraging them to keep on begging?

93. If I lose my memory am I the same person?

94. If I acquire your memory who am I then?

95. If I save a life with one hand but take a life with the other at exactly the same time, am I a good person or a bad one?

96. Is a good person a good person when they are asleep?

97. IS A LEAF ON THE TREE OR PART OF THE TREE?

98. Does a tree weigh less when you take one leaf from it?

99. Is a wooden table still a tree?

100. If I chop a tree down and start writing on it does it become a table? What if I don't chop it down but climb up it and start writing on it?

101. If I take a photo of a photo of you, do I have a photo of you or a photo of a photo of you?

102. *Could I pay for a bunch of bananas with a bunch of bananas?*

103. CAN I BUY A POUND FROM YOU FOR A POUND?

104. If I stick a bunch of flowers in a computer does the computer become a vase?

105. If I stick a bunch of flowers in my mouth do I become a vase?

106. If I fill a vase with concrete is it still a vase? What if I fill it with flowers?

107. *Is the hole in the middle part of the vase?*

108. IF BOTH HANDS FALL OFF MY CLOCK IS IT STILL A CLOCK?

109. *Do you make your own hair?*

110. *If I paint over a window is it still a window?*

111. Can you feel guilty for something you haven't done?

112. Can you be racist against your own race?

113. Can a non-racist person tell a racist joke?

114. CAN A BLIND PERSON BE RACIST?

115. *Is a pound worth more to a poor person than a rich person?*

116. Would you play the Lottery if there was more chance of winning but also of losing everything?

117. If you had a box with a button on it that, when pressed, meant someone anywhere in the world would experience pain but no one would ever know it was you, would you press it? Would you do it for £1,000,000?

118. *Would you do it if someone somewhere experienced something wonderful at the same time as someone was experiencing something bad?*

119. Where does your lap start?

120. Where does the sky start?

121. Are clouds in, under or above the sky?

122. DOES A CUP OF TEA WEIGH MORE WHEN YOU ADD A SPOONFUL OF SUGAR?

123. *Can you weigh the sky? Would it be heavier on a cloudy day?*

124. If I sucked all the colour out of the room what would the room look like?

125. Is silence a sound? Can you hear silence?

126. If a lion could talk would we be able to understand it? (Thanks to Mr Wittgenstein again for that one.)

127. *Can a fly see a skyscraper?*

128. IS THE MUSH INSIDE A CHRYSALIS ALIVE OR DEAD? WHAT ABOUT THE YOLK IN AN EGG?

129. If I knew your genetic make-up and knew you were going to die at a certain age would you want me to tell you? Should I tell you anyway? Would you want anyone else to know? Would you want anyone else specifically not to know?

130. *If the US is the most powerful nation on earth should the rest of the world get to vote in the US elections?*

131. Was the wheel or the box mankind's greatest invention? If neither, then what?

132. Is love an invention created by humans?

133. *What's the most important part of a fork? A box? A dog?*

134. WHICH IS THE GREATEST TECHNOLOGICAL INNOVATION – THE FIRST AEROPLANE OR THE LATEST ONE?

135. Is a house a work of art? A brick? A box? Graffiti? School uniform? A spider's web?

136. *How many bricks is a wall?*

137. If I have a problem with my brain that makes me do bad things am I a bad person? If I have an operation and that problem gets removed, so I no longer do bad things, am I a good or bad person? Was I a bad person?

138. With a water shortage looming could you harvest puddles? Who owns the water in them?

139. If I tell a joke that is translated who is making the other person laugh – me or the translator?

140. Can a dog be kind?

141. Is the cuckoo a 'bad' bird?

142. *Is a bird singing or talking?*

143. ARE YOU IN THE ROOM OR PART OF THE ROOM? SCHOOL? COUNTRY? WORLD? UNIVERSE?

144. If you changed your name would it change who you were? Would the old you still exist?

145. Can you stand on the same beach twice? (Think long-shore drift ...)

146. IF YOU FILL A ROOM FULL OF BRICKS IS IT STILL A ROOM?

147. *If you take the ceiling off a room is it still a room?*

148. Can a sheet of red paper be blank?

149. <u>Is the moon in the sky?</u>

150. *Is 'be neutral towards thy neighbour' better than 'love thy neighbour'?*

151. If a robot had a human brain, would it go to heaven? (Thanks to Bart Simpson for that one.)

152. *Do birds fly through the sky, in the sky or under the sky? If 'in', do they displace it as they go through it? If so, is there less sky when birds migrate? And where does the sky get displaced to?*

153. Where do thoughts come from?

154. *Does a goldfish know it's your pet? Could it think it was the other way round? Could it think you were its slave?*

155. Do computers think? What about clocks?

156. Can anything be a toy? Can anything definitely not be a toy?

157. Can animals be naughty?

158. Do animals have feelings? All animals? All feelings?

159. Do animals have rights? All animals? All rights?

160. IF I SHOUT AT YOU TO PROTECT YOU AM I YOUR FRIEND?

161. Can you be friends and not friends with someone at the same time?

162. *Can you like and not like something or someone at the same time?*

163. Where does the air come from when you inflate a tyre?

164. *If I discovered a cure for cancer but didn't want to share my discovery with the world, should I be made to? How could I be made to?*

165. If I walk up a path and then back down it, does that count as one walk or two?

166. Is it OK if I swear at you in a language that you don't understand? What if it is a language that I have made up?

167. *If a fly travelling east hits a train travelling west does the fly stop for a fraction of a second as it changes direction? If so, as it is in contact with the train when this happens, does the train stop too? So, does the fly stop the train?*

168. There's a 1 in 3 million chance of being hit by lightning in the UK. If the person next to you gets hit during a storm does that mean then that you are now safer, more at risk, or just the same?

169. Do I weigh less when I spit?

170. Does air weigh anything? If it does, do I weigh less when I pass wind?

171. WHAT DOES THE BACK OF A RAINBOW LOOK LIKE?

172. Can you step on water?

173. Can you prove that all ravens are black?

174. TRIGGER'S BROOM HAS HAD 17 NEW HEADS AND 14 NEW HANDLES BUT IS IT STILL THE SAME BROOM?

175. How many horns does a unicorn have?

176. *If you picture a flagpole a mile away and then measure the distance between you and it in your imagination, would it be a mile long?*

177. Do ideas come from inside or outside your head?

178. Do animals have ideas?

179. WHICH IS THE MORE FUTILE THING TO DO, STAND ON A LADDER TO TRY AND TOUCH A STAR OR MAKE A WISH?

180. Is it ever possible to learn nothing?

181. *Can you stop thinking?*

182. *Are thoughts and memories the same thing?*

183. Is happiness something you find or
something you have?

184. *Which has the most freedom, an ant or
a schoolchild?*

185. Could you ever build a computer that knows
everything?

186. COULD A COMPUTER EVER BE HAPPY?

187. If you always got everything you ever wished for would you be always be happy?

188. Can being sad bring you pleasure?

189. If cars could be controlled by PlayStation®-like controls should children be allowed to drive? (Once they've passed their virtual driving tests of course)

190. *Is it possible that our universe is contained in a speck of dust on the back of a large goat?*

191. If a bully threatens you should you cry and scream like a baby so they don't bother, or be big and strong and let them hit you?

192. HOW DO YOU KNOW YOU HAVE A HEAD?

193. Can anybody make you do something, whether you want to or not?

194. CAN YOU BEND AIR?

195. Does electricity weigh anything?

196. *Does a dog know it's a dog?*

197. Am I any less alive when I'm asleep?

198. *Is 0 degrees a temperature? Is 0 cm a height or 0 years an age?*

199. IS A WHITE SHEET OF PAPER MORE BLANK THAN A BLACK SHEET OF PAPER?

200. *If Manchester United and Chelsea swapped all their players which would be the team in blue?*

201. I can make traffic lights turn from red to green just by staring at them – true or false?

202. DO DOGS BELIEVE IN GOD? DO COMPUTERS BELIEVE IN GOD? DO MARTIANS BELIEVE IN GOD?

203. Are the English word 'international' and the French word 'international' the same word?

204. Does the back of a firework look the same as the front?

205. *Which is more real, a table or love? Manchester United or Ryan Giggs? James Bond or Princess Diana? Time or Jupiter? Thoughts or feelings? Elephants or eyelash mites? Air or fire?*

206. If the further you are away from me the smaller your head looks, how close do you have to be to me before your head is its actual size?

207. *Who owns your e-mail inbox when you die?*

208. WHO DOES THE METRO, A
FREE NEWSPAPER, BELONG TO
WHEN YOU'RE READING IT?

209. If I play chess against my computer and I lose,
who or what beat me?

210. *Can a bed communicate?*

211. *Is a tree that has been chopped down but still flowers in the spring dead or alive? What about a bunch of roses in a vase? A Christmas tree in your house?*

212. Is it natural to be greedy? If so, is being greedy OK then?

213. Do you think your bedroom exists, believe your bedroom exists, know your bedroom exists or something else?

214. When you comb your hair, is it art?

215. When you are scared by a scary film, is the fear real or imaginary?

216. IF A BABY GREW UP ALL ALONE ON A DESERT ISLAND WOULD IT KNOW RIGHT FROM WRONG? GOOD FROM BAD? UP FROM DOWN?

217. When does loud start?

218. *Is there a time lag between seeing a tree and realising that you have seen a tree?*

219. Is something boring because of it or because of you?

220. Which is the more important invention – the telescope or the microscope?

221. WHEN YOU SPEAK TO SOMEONE ON THE PHONE IS IT THE OTHER PERSON SPEAKING OR THE PHONE?

222. *Who owns your fingerprints?*

223. Is water porous?

224. *Is soup a food or a drink? Do you drink it or eat it? What about melted ice cream? Jelly?*

225. Can you remember something you haven't done or that hasn't happened?

226. *If I gave you lump of mud to play with would it be a toy? If yes, would it be a toy when you stopped playing with it? Was it a toy before you started playing with it?*

227. IS A TOY CAR THAT NO ONE HAS EVER PLAYED WITH STILL A TOY?

228. Could you have an invisible toy?

229. *Can you have a conversation with an invisible friend?*

230. If I smell cheese, does that mean there are tiny bits of the cheese up my nose? What about if I smell your feet? Or worse ...?

231. Does everything have a taste?

232. Can you dream of a taste?

233. If I'm being kind to you but end up hurting you, was I kind or not?

234. If I'm being kind to you but you think I'm being horrible, am I being kind or not?

235. Can you trust a dog? A mouse? A chair?

236. Does your house weigh more the dustier it gets?

237. *If I make a tree out of wood, is it more like a tree than one made of plastic?*

238. CAN YOU HAVE A THIRD OF LOVE?

239. CAN YOU LOVE SOMEONE BUT NOT LIKE THEM?

240. Can you love someone and hate them at the same time?

241. *Should stupid people be allowed to vote?*

242. IF YOU FEED A TERRORIST, DOES THAT MAKE YOU A TERRORIST?

243. If scientists could create a new species of animal purely for testing medicines on, should they use it for that purpose?

244. *If you steal my pen and I steal yours in return am I a thief too? Am I the same as you? Does it work for all crimes?*

245. Is perfume a work of art?

246. *If I deliberately drop a bucket of paint onto a canvas is that art? What if I do it and get exactly the same result but it was an accident?*

247. If all religions were banned, would there be more or less war in the world?

248. IS WAR A GOOD THING?

249. Could you have war without anyone dying?

250. If dropping litter is a bad thing, would it be better if I bury my Mars® wrappers in the ground like the council does?

251. *If a new baby comes into your family is it loved more, less or the same as the other family members? If the same or more, where does the extra love come from?*

252. DO YOU LOVE A FAMILY MEMBER MORE, THE SAME OR LESS AFTER THEY HAVE DIED?

253. Could a dog be rich? A baby? A pen?

254. Do you think when you're asleep?

255. IS LIFE AN EXPERIMENT?

256. *If you found a contraceptive in your child's room, should you be pleased?*

257. Is it the same road in both directions?

258. *Is a dead horse a horse?*[8]

259. Why don't dogs laugh? Is it because they don't have a sense of humour?

---

[8] Early last century a horsebox was allowed to travel up to 30 mph but a meat wagon was limited to 20 mph.

260. *Is Marmite nice – yes or no?*

Bibliography

101 Philosophy Problems, second edition. Martin Cohen, Routledge, London, 1999

A Short Treatise on the Great Virtues, Andre Comte-Sponville, William Heineman, London, 2002

But Why?: Developing Philosophical Thinking in the Classroom, Sara Stanley with Steve Bowkett, Network Educational Press, London, 2004

Smart Moves: Why Learning Is Not All in Your Head, Clara Hannaford, Ph.D., Great River Books, Utah, 2005

Teaching Thinking, Robert Fisher, Continuum, London, 2003

The Consolations of Philosophy, Boethius, The Folio Society, London, 1998

The Mind's Eye, Douglas R Hofstadter and Daniel C Dennet, Penguin, London, 1982

The Tao of Pooh, Benjamin Hoff, Methuen, London, 1982

Think, Simon Blackburn, Oxford University Press, Oxford, 1999

Zen and the Art of Motorcycle Maintenance, Robert M Pirsig, Vintage, London, 1974

Useful websites

www.independentthinking.co.uk
Ideas and resources for thinking, learning and motivation from Ian Gilbert's company.

www.independentthinkingpress.com
Books from some of the UK's leading educational innovators.

www.philosophy-foundation.org/
An educational charity supporting philosophical enquiry in the classroom.

www.sapere.org.uk
Training and support for developing your skills in Philosophy for Children.

www.thunks.co.uk
Online forum for discussing Thunks and contributing your own (see page 22).

Index to the *Thunks*